# Note to Parents

Favorite activities and games are a happy part of every beach outing. *Sand in Your Shoes* has been designed to enhance the fun. Activities vary from simple sand and water play for the youngest children to more complicated games and projects for older children. Of course, safety tips for swimming and water play are included. The Jiminy Cricket symbol appears with these safety cautions and with any projects that require adult help.

The beach outing is a preparation for swimming. Tots splashing in the shallowest water are getting used to the cool, wet feeling of their faces and bodies. Older children ducking with a beach ball are having fun—and also experiencing their natural buoyancy in water.

Help your child avoid chill and fatigue by alternating fun in the water with fun on the sand. And when active games on the sand become too heated, try a few quiet games before going back into the water.

You will want to be with children when they are in the water, of course—but join in the sand play, as well. Try helping build those sand castles! Children will delight in your participation—and you will have fun, too.

# Sand
# in Your Shoes

## Fun at the Beach

Published by
World Book Encyclopedia, Inc.
a Scott Fetzer company
Chicago

# Donald's Wild Ride

"Surprise!" squealed Huey.

"Smile for—" shouted Dewey.

"—the birdie!" chortled Louie.

"Oh, no," groaned Donald, opening his eyes. He had been having a beautiful dream about surfing—about riding the big one.

"Gotcha!" yelled Huey, Dewey, and Louie as three cameras clicked.

"Don't you know it's not polite to take pictures when people aren't expecting it?" Donald grumbled.

Huey, Dewey, and Louie just grinned.

"Unexpected pictures—" said Huey.

"—are the best pictures," said Dewey.

"It says so in our book," said Louie.

"Well, I wish the writer of that book had talked to me about politeness," said Donald. "I could teach him a thing or two about that! From now on, *ask* before you snap someone's picture. And no more pictures until I give the word."

"Okay, Unca Donald," sighed Huey.

"Whatever you say," sighed Dewey.

"We'll wait for the word," sighed Louie.

4

Suddenly there was a noise at the end of the beach. People spilled out of cars and buses. A TV van pulled up. A crew with cameras and microphones got out.

"Have you seen him yet?" called someone.

"Seen who?" asked Donald.

"Duzzy, the sea monster," said someone else. "Does he or doesn't he exist—that's why he's called *Duzzy.*"

"Ho-ho, yuckety-yuckety," everyone laughed.

A TV announcer poked a microphone at Donald. "It's said that Duzzy appears every year at this time—but nobody's ever actually seen him. Have you seen him today, sir?" the announcer asked.

"Seen a sea monster!" exploded Donald. "If you want my opinion, I'll tell you: There's no such thing as sea monsters. They aren't real. Sea monsters are figments of the imagination!"

"So you don't believe in Duzzy," said the announcer.

"Not in Duzzy or Fuzzy or Wuzzy!" said Donald. "You can watch for sea monsters all you want. We're gonna go have fun in the sun. Come on, guys."

He led Huey, Dewey, and Louie to the far end of the beach, where there weren't any people. As they followed, Huey, Dewey, and Louie looked back at the crowd.

"I kinda wish there was a sea monster," said Huey.

"It might be a really nice sea monster and want to be friends," said Dewey.

"It might even be a leftover kind of dinosaur," said Louie.

"Lotta nonsense," Donald muttered. "The make-believe stuff people swallow boggles my mind."

There really was a lot to do at the beach, even without sea monsters. And all of it was fun. After lunch Donald told Huey, Dewey, and Louie to play quietly for a while. "It's wise not to swim too soon after you eat," he said.

So while Donald had another little nap, Huey, Dewey, and Louie wrote a note. They sealed it in a bottle and tossed it far out into the water.

"Maybe someone will find it," said Huey.

"Someone far away," said Dewey.

"And write back," said Louie.

Late in the afternoon, the crowd at the end of the
beach climbed into their cars and left. The TV crew got
into their van and went away, waving. "Maybe we'll be
luckier next year," they called.

"No, you won't. Sea monsters are just somebody's idea
of a joke," Donald called back.

"Well, I'm going in for one last dip before we go
home," he told Huey, Dewey, and Louie. "Don't get in
any trouble while I'm gone." He swam out toward the
diving raft, splashing mightily.

Suddenly there was a great lifting of waves around
him. The waves raised him in a big SWOOOOSH—and
he found himself on top of a huge body.

"Hey!" he yelled. "Put me down!"

A giant head lifted out of the water and turned to
look at him with an impish grin. "Who says I'm
somebody's idea of a joke!" burbled a soft, watery-
sounding voice. And Duzzy sped off across the bay—
with Donald on his back.

"Help!" yelled Donald, hanging on for dear life.

Duzzy whizzed completely around the bay faster than Donald could say "figment of the imagination."

"Whoa!" yelled Donald as they streaked past Huey, Dewey, and Louie.

"I believe in you! I believe you're real! You *do* exist!" Donald yelled as they whizzed around the bay a second time.

"Lights!" yelled Huey.

"Cameras!" yelled Dewey.

"Wow! What action!" yelled Louie. *Click . . . click . . . click* went their three cameras.

"I believe!" Donald shouted into the wind and spray as they whizzed around again. "I belieeeeeeeve!"

Duzzy slowed down in front of the beach. Donald slid off his back and splashed toward shore. Duzzy grinned at Huey, Dewey, and Louie. He flipped his long tail one last time and dived underwater.

"We took your picture even though you didn't give us the word," said Huey. "Is that okay?"

"Did you ask Duzzy if he's a leftover dinosaur?" asked Dewey.

"Were you scared?" asked Louie.

"Me, scared?" asked Donald. "Why, that was almost as good as riding a bucking bronco when I was a cowboy. And no, I didn't ask him if he's a leftover dinosaur. It's not polite to ask personal questions. And yes, it was okay to take my picture."

Later, after the picture of Donald riding Duzzy was in the paper, a strange letter came for Huey, Dewey, and Louie. It was in a bottle. In watery-looking writing, it said:

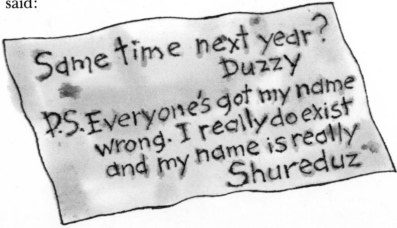

Same time next year?
Duzzy
P.S. Everyone's got my name wrong. I really do exist and my name is really Shureduz

# Getting into the Swim

Huey, Dewey, and Louie liked to play in the water. They floated their toy boats. They played *Frog and Polliwogs*. But they wanted to swim.

"We could have lots more fun—" said Huey.

"—in the water—" said Dewey.

"—if we could swim," said Louie.

Donald heard them. That very day he gave them their first swimming lesson. And they did have more fun!

Here are the things they learned to do. You can try them, too.

Sit down in water that comes up to your knees. Lean back on your elbows. Your legs will float to the top. Your whole body wants to float like a boat.

Lie on your stomach, chin up, with your hands on the bottom. Walk on your hands and let your legs float behind you.

Stand in water that comes up to your waist. Bend your knees until your shoulders are underwater. You'll feel the water press against the air in your chest. The air in your chest helps you float.

With your knees bent, bounce on your feet for a minute. Can you feel how your body bobs in the water? You feel lighter in water than you do on land.

Jiminy Cricket says, "When you are learning to swim, always have a grown-up with you."

Hold your breath. Lean over and put your face in the water. Can you do this three times? Face in 1 . . . 2 . . . 3!

# Safety First

"What a great day for swimming," Donald said. "I can't wait to get into that water! Come on, Daisy—I'll race you!"

"Wait a minute, Donald," Daisy said. "Let's check with the lifeguard before we go in."

"I'm glad you asked," the lifeguard said. "That part of the beach *looks* safe, but there are sharp rocks beneath the water. Let me give you some safety tips."

1. **Pay attention to warning signs.** They were put up for a good reason.
2. **Never swim alone.** Always have a buddy with you.
3. **Never swim in lonely places.** Be sure a lifeguard or a grown-up swimmer is nearby.
4. **Stay in shallow water until you are able to swim at least 75 feet (22.5 meters) and feel good about it.**
5. **Don't ride floating rafts or rings into deep water.** If they lose air, you will sink.
6. **Don't go in the water right after eating or playing hard.** You may get dangerous muscle cramps.
7. **If the water is too cold to be comfortable, don't swim.**
8. **If the bottom has rocks or holes, know where they are.** And find out where shallow water ends and deep water begins before you swim.

Jiminy Cricket says, "Never call for help unless you really need it!"

 "Okay?" asked the lifeguard.
 "You bet," Donald answered. "Come on, Daisy. Let's find a safe spot to swim!"

# Sandmen and Hand Trees

Huey, Dewey, and Louie took lots of things to the beach when they were small—pails and shovels, pencils (old ones), plastic straws, and plastic cups and containers of every shape and size. They also took buttons and spools, paper towel tubes, and even a little flag!

Can you guess what they did with them? All kinds of wonderful things!

Huey used his pail to carry water. He wet the sand and made sandmen. He used a pencil to trace their faces, and he gave them soda-straw arms.

Dewey made a city with houses and roads. He made a tunnel with the paper towel tube. He put toy cars on the roads. The pond is a plastic cup filled with water.

Louie made a hand tree. He used his shovel to draw the trunk. He watered the sand at the top of the tree and pressed his hands into the wet sand to make leaf prints.

Together, Huey and Dewey and Louie made a sand castle. It had towers and a wall, a moat, and even a flag on the tallest tower.

Jiminy Cricket says, "Help keep your beach clean. When you bring your things to the beach to play, take them home at the end of the day."

# A Boat Afloat

What floats?

A leaf floats. So Huey, Dewey, and Louie made boats of leaves. The leaf boats floated until they got soaked. Then they sank.

Paper floats—for a while. So Huey, Dewey, and Louie made boats of paper. The paper boats floated until the paper soaked up water. Then they sank, too.

At last, Huey, Dewey, and Louie found a way to make boats that didn't soak up water. They made milk-carton boats. Those boats floated.

You can make boats that float, too.

## What you'll need

Clean, empty milk cartons    Knife
Masking tape or stapler    Paper plate
Old greeting card (large)

### Huey's Flat-Bottomed Boat

1. Cut one long side off a milk carton. Tape or staple the spout closed.

2. Cut matching slits on both sides of the boat, about one quarter of the way back from the spout, for your sail. Use a paper plate for the sail.

### Dewey's and Louie's Side-by-Side Sailboat

1. Cut downward through one edge of the carton, from top to bottom corner.

2. Keep cutting diagonally across the bottom to the opposite corner. Then make the same kind of cut across the top.

3. Gently fold the carton open. Cut a slit on the center fold, about one quarter of the way back. Stick a large, colorful greeting card in it for a sail.

Jiminy Cricket says, "Ask a grown-up to help you cut the cartons."

17

# Let's Go Swimming

Huey, Dewey, and Louie were happy as tadpoles. They opened their eyes and looked around underwater. They had contests to see who could pick up the most things from around their feet.

"Playing in the water—" said Huey.

"—is more fun than playing—" said Dewey.

"—in the sand," said Louie.

Daisy laughed. "Now I know it's time for your next swimming lesson," she said.

**The Jellyfish**

Stand in water up to your waist. Put your head underwater and lean down as though to touch your toes. Your feet will come off the bottom. Let your arms and legs dangle. When you're tired of being a jellyfish, just stand up.

## The Back Float

Lean back in the water, your arms out to the side. Push lightly with your feet. Your legs will float upward. Let your legs and hips come to the top of the water. Paddle your hands gently.

To stand, bring your knees up to your chest and drop your feet to the bottom.

## The Face Float

Hold your arms straight above your head, bend over, and put your face in the water. Lean forward and push with your feet. Your legs will lift and float behind you.

When you're tired of floating, pull your knees forward to your chest, drop your feet to the bottom, and stand up.

Jiminy Cricket says, "Have a grown-up with you when you are learning to swim. And always float toward shallow water or the shore. Never float toward deep water."

19

# Water Fun

"And now," said wise old Uncle Donald, "let me show you how to play fastest-on-the-draw. Did you wash out your squirt bottles at home?"

"You bet," said Huey.

"We wouldn't want—" said Dewey.

"—to pollute the lake with soap," said Louie.

"Right," said Donald. "Now, fill your bottles with water and screw on the top. Drop your hand to your side, and when you're ready—"

"Ready!" yelled Huey, Dewey, and Louie.

Guess who was fastest on the draw!

Here are some more water games to play.

## Bullfrog and Polliwogs

Let one player be the bullfrog. Polliwogs stand in the water, each
with hands on the hips of the polliwog in front. At Go, the bullfrog
tries to tag a polliwog and the line of polliwogs tries to dodge.
When the bullfrog tags a polliwog, they change places.

## Sandy Hands

Have everyone sit in a row in shallow water. The first player scoops
up a handful of wet sand and passes it to the second player, who
passes it on. The last player drops it in a bucket. How long will it
take to fill the pail? With enough players, two teams can race.

## Duck Ball

Kneel in a circle in the water. Pass a ball around the circle. When
you get it, you must duck underwater and come up before passing
the ball to the next player.

# Beach Fun

Fish watched from way out in the bay. Birds watched, wheeling and dipping in the sky. A turtle watched from his lookout on a log.

They were watching Donald and Daisy and the boys play noisy games on the beach—and they were wishing they could play.

But the fish had to stay in their school . . . and the birds had to stay in the sky . . . and the turtle had to look after his log.

Here are some beach games to play.

### Toad Go Home

Dig a row of five holes in the sand, about a foot (30 centimeters) apart. Dig another hole, *Home,* about five feet (1.5 meters) behind the row. Mark a base line in front of the row.

Take turns tossing pebbles from the base line into the holes. The first person to score 25 points wins.

You can make 25 points in one turn by calling, "Toad, go home!" and tossing the pebble into Home. If you miss, you lose your next turn. A pebble into Home doesn't count if you forget to call "Toad, go home!"

### Volleyball

Don't forget to take a beach ball—you can play volleyball with it. If you don't have a net, make a "people net" with players standing in a row, holding hands. Of course, you should change the net from time to time!

### Sand Fleas

Smooth out a large area of sand. Then "walk" a large wagon wheel in the cleared area—a circle crossed by spokes. Pick someone to be *It.*

Everyone, including *It,* hops like sand fleas, staying on the circle or one of its spokes. *It* tries to tag the fleas. Anyone who is tagged, or who hops off the wheel or a spoke, becomes *It.*

# Umbrella Games

"Ooooo, but it's hot," said Daisy. "We've all been playing so hard! Come sit with me under the umbrella. Let's play some umbrella games."

Umbrella games are quiet, sit-down-and-cool-off games. Some of them have winners. Some are just things that are fun to do.

Here are some of Daisy's favorite umbrella games. You don't even need an umbrella to play them!

## I Came to the Beach

This is a word game. The leader starts a list by saying, for example, "I came to the beach and I brought my yellow duck." The next player repeats the sentence and adds one thing, such as "my goldfish" or "my swim fins." The game continues with each player adding to the list. Players who miss are out. When everyone misses, start a new list!

## Unload the Boat

Gather pebbles, twigs, blades of grass, shells—any small objects you can find on the beach. Draw a boat shape in the sand. Pile in the beach gatherings willy-nilly to fill the boat.

Now try to remove one thing at a time without disturbing any other object. If you accidentally move something, it's the next player's turn.

## Wiggle Tiggle

Sit in a circle. Choose one person to lead. The leader does one thing—for example, wiggles his nose. The second player does the same thing and adds another action, such as wiggle the nose and tug one ear. Each player repeats the last player's actions and adds one more. When someone misses, the players call "Wiggle tiggle out," and that person drops out. The last player left is the winner.

# Sand, Wind, and Water

## By the Sea

I started early, took my dog,
And visited the sea;
The mermaids in the basement
Came out to look at me,

And frigates in the upper floor
Extended hempen hands,
Presuming me to be a mouse
Aground, upon the sands.

Emily Dickinson

## Bobby Shaftoe

Bobby Shaftoe's gone to sea,
Silver buckles at his knee;
He'll come back and marry me,
  Pretty Bobby Shaftoe.

Bobby Shaftoe's fat and fair
Combing down his yellow hair,
He's my love forevermore,
  Pretty Bobby Shaftoe.

       Nursery Rhyme

## Ferry Me
## Across the Water

"Ferry me across the water,
  Do, boatman, do."
"If you've a penny in your purse
  I'll ferry you."

"I have a penny in my purse,
  And my eyes are blue;
So ferry me across the water,
  Do, boatman, do."

"Step into my ferry-boat,
  Be they black or blue,
And for the penny in your purse
  I'll ferry you."

       Christina Rossetti

27

# Swim Like a Fish

Here are some of the things Donald and Daisy know about sandy, watery places.

They know that ocean water is salty. And they know that water in lakes is not salty.

They know that the oceans have tides—the water is high on the beach part of the day and low on the beach for a part of the day. And they know that lakes do not have tides.

Donald and Daisy like to put on face masks and look around underwater. They like to see things as the fish see them.

In the ocean, along a rocky shore, Donald sees mussels that open to let water—and tiny bits of food—flow through. He sees limpets and periwinkles, too. Seaweed floats near him like a soft green scarf. He looks down and sees a sand dollar lying on the bottom—and a crab crawling nearby.

In the soft green light of the lake, Daisy sees small fish. A piece of driftwood is half-buried in the sand. A turtle hides near a rock. Daisy looks up and sees a leaf floating on the water. The surface of the water is like a shiny mirror.

# A Window in the Water

"I wish I could look around underwater," said Huey. "I mean really—like a fish or a turtle."

"I open my eyes underwater," said Dewey, "but it's hard to see things clearly."

"That's 'cause we're used to seeing in air, not water," said Louie. "Unca Donald told me that."

Donald heard them talking. "I know a way for you to look around underwater," he said. He showed them how to make water windows.

After that, Huey, Dewey, and Louie *could* look around underwater—just like fish or turtles.

Jiminy Cricket says, "Plastic can be tough. Ask a grown-up to help you cut the hole in the bucket."

**What you'll need**

Old plastic bucket

Clear plastic bag or food wrap

String or rubber band

Tape

Scissors

1. Cut a hole in the bottom of the bucket.

2. Cut a piece of clear plastic big enough to cover the large end of the bucket. Fasten the plastic in place with string or a rubber band. Then tape the plastic down tightly so that no water can leak in.

3. Using both hands, lower your water window partway into the water, plastic side down. (Don't let any water run over the top into the bucket.) You will find that you see underwater things clearly with your water window. Your water window makes things look larger, too.

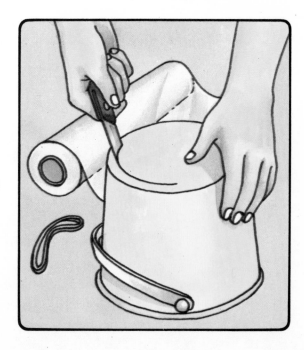

# Fun in the Sand

Donald and Daisy were at the beach. Daisy wanted to read. Donald wanted to *do* something.

So while Daisy read her book, Donald made a sand sculpture. He turned Daisy into a mermaid.

Mermaid Daisy was happy. She was reading. And Sculptor Donald was happy, too. He was *doing* something!

You can make a sand sculpture of Donald's face. Just follow the directions on the next page. Then make some sand sculptures of your own.

**What you'll need**

Pail
Shovel
Plastic containers
Ice-cream sticks

Trowel
Old spoons, spatula, and
    other kitchen utensils

Jiminy Cricket says, "Keep your tools in one special place where nobody will step on them."

1. Carry water to the sandy place where you will make your sculpture. Wet the sand and smooth it with a spatula or flat stick.

2. Draw an outline of Donald's head in the sand. Most of Donald's head is a circle. Mound up sand inside the circle and pat it into a smooth rounded hump. Keep the sand damp while you work—sprinkle it with water often.

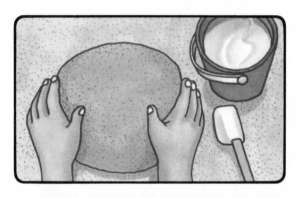

3. Add two rounded ovals for Donald's eyes. Build up two smaller rounded shapes inside them for the center of his eyes.

4. Add two long, curved shapes, side by side, in the lower half of Donald's face. Pat and smooth the shapes into Donald's mouth.

5. Use a stick to draw the other markings on Donald's face.

"What are dog days?" asked Huey. "Nobody ever talks about dog days during the winter."

"Maybe it means there are more dogs at the beach on those days," said Dewey.

"Maybe it means dogs get a free swim at the pool on those days," said Louie.

"Dog days are hot, uncomfortable days in July and August," Daisy told them. "That's when the dog star, Sirius, rises with the sun. That's why these days are called dog days."

"And everybody—" said Huey.

"—goes to the beach—" said Dewey.

"—to cool off," said Louie.

Huey, Dewey, and Louie made a sand sculpture of Pluto to celebrate dog days.

## What you'll need

Sand pail
Shovel
Plastic containers

Ice-cream stick
Spatula and other tools
  for modeling

1. Smooth and wet an area of sand. With a stick, draw an outline of Pluto's head.

2. Fill the big areas first. The back part of Pluto's head is a circle. Mound sand into a smooth, rounded shape. Then build a rounded pipe shape for Pluto's neck and a half-moon shape for his mouth and nose. Keep the sand wet. Sprinkle it with water often.

3. Now build the smaller parts of the face—ovals for Pluto's eyes, smaller circles for the pupils, and a long teardrop shape for Pluto's nearest ear. Part of a teardrop shows under his chin for his other ear. Add a circle of sand for the tip of his nose.

4. With a stick, draw the lines that will finish Pluto's face.

Jiminy Cricket says, "Keep your tools in your sand pail when you aren't using them, so that nobody will step on them."

35

# Beachcombers

"What are you guys doing?" asked Donald.

"We're being beachcombers," said Huey.

"We're combing the sand—" said Dewey.

"—into pretty patterns," said Louie.

Huey, Dewey, and Louie had made sand combs to bring to the beach. They were making interesting marks and patterns in the sand.

"Well, you're combing the beach, that's true," said Donald. "But beachcombing usually means something else. Beachcombers are folks who wander around on the beach finding exciting things.

"So you guys comb the beach your way. I'm going off to be a beachcomber my way. Who knows what I'll find for my collection!"

Donald found a piece of
driftwood. The sand and
water had rubbed it smooth,
and the sun had made it an
interesting color. It has an
unusual shape, so Donald
saved it.

Donald found these shells
along the seashore. He'll add
them to his shell collection.

Donald found these colored
stones on a sandy shore. When
they dried off, they lost some
of their pretty color. So
Donald rubbed them lightly
with baby oil to bring out the
color and make them shine.

Donald found a small friend,
too—a tiny crab. But he didn't
take it home! He knew that it
needed to live on the sandy
shore. So he watched it until it
scurried away.

# Make a Beach Kite

"It's fun to run on the beach," said Huey. "The sand feels squooshy under my feet."

"When I run, I feel the wind on my face," said Dewey. "That's why I like to play tag."

"Running to make my kite go up is the most fun of all," said Louie. "You should try it!"

Huey and Dewey flew Louie's kite—and it *was* fun. So they made kites just like Louie's to take to the beach.

You can make a beach kite, too. Then you can feel the sand all squooshy under your feet and the wind cool on your face, and you can watch your kite sail overhead.

## What you'll need

2 sticks each 20 inches (51 cm) long    Rags
Felt-tip or china markers    Ruler
Plastic bag    Scissors
String    Tape

Jiminy Cricket says, "Ask a grown-up to help you measure and cut the kite shape."

1. Cut the plastic bag down one side and across the bottom. Spread the bag out flat. Measure and cut a piece of plastic 25 inches (64 cm) wide and 20 inches (51 cm) long.

2. Next, fold the plastic in half. On the top and bottom edges, measure 7½ inches (19 cm) from the fold and make a mark.

3. Measure 9 inches (23 cm) diagonally from the top mark to the edge of the bag opposite the fold. Make a mark there.

4. Draw lines to connect the side mark with the top and bottom marks. Cut through both layers of plastic, following the lines.

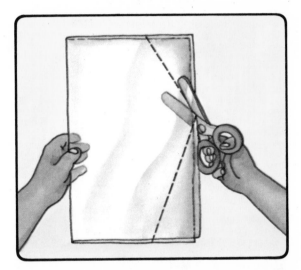

5. Unfold the plastic and tape the sticks to the kite shape, as shown. Add more tape at the corners, where the string will attach to the kite. Cut holes through the tape.

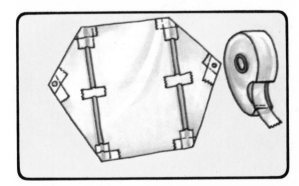

6. Cut a bridle string 3 inches (8 cm) longer than the distance between holes. Push one end through each hole, back to front, and tie the string to the corners.

7. Fasten your ball of flying string to the center of the bridle string.

8. Tape some rag tails to the bottom of your kite. Now try your kite. You can add or take away tails until it flies steadily.

# Good Night, Mateys

The sun was setting. The sky was turning red and gold.
A red-and-gold path of sunshine rippled across the
water.

"Well, mates," said Captain Donald, "it's time to head
for home."

So Huey, Dewey, and Louie sang, "Good night,
mateys, good night, mateys, good night, mateys, we're
going to leave you now. Merrily we roll along. . . ."

And they sang good night to every single thing on the
beach!

# The Eentsy Weentsy Spider

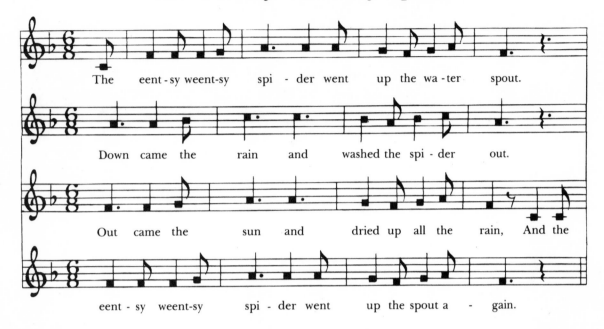

The eent-sy weent-sy spi-der went up the wa-ter spout.

Down came the rain and washed the spi-der out.

Out came the sun and dried up all the rain, And the

eent-sy weent-sy spi-der went up the spout a - gain.

# Old MacDonald

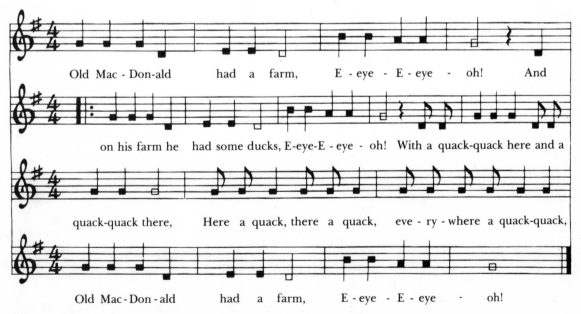

Old Mac-Don-ald had a farm, E - eye - E - eye - oh! And

on his farm he had some ducks, E-eye-E-eye-oh! With a quack-quack here and a

quack-quack there, Here a quack, there a quack, eve-ry-where a quack-quack,

Old Mac-Don-ald had a farm, E - eye - E - eye - oh!

Some other animals on Old MacDonald's farm are:
  Chicks (With a chick-chick here . . .)
  Pigs (With an oink-oink here . . .)

Cows (With a moo-moo here . . .)
Donkeys (With a hee-haw here . . .)
Sheep (With a baa-baa here . . .)

Some of these songs are rounds. To sing a round, let one singer or group begin the song. When the first group reaches *, the next group begins at the beginning.

## Row, Row, Row Your Boat

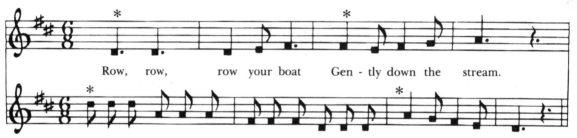

## Three Blind Mice

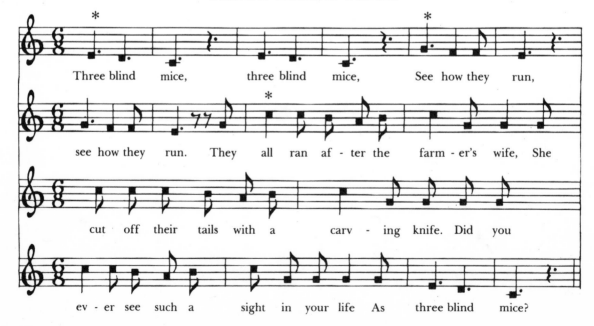

# Oh, How Lovely Is the Evening

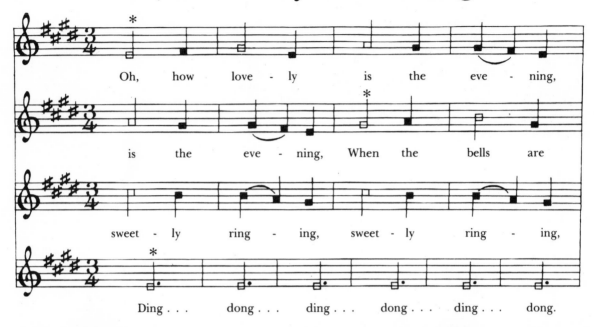

Oh, how love - ly is the eve - ning,

is the eve - ning, When the bells are

sweet - ly ring - ing, sweet - ly ring - ing,

Ding . . . dong . . . ding . . . dong . . . . ding . . . dong.

# Hush, Little Baby

Hush, lit-tle ba-by, don't say a word, Ma-ma's going to buy you a mock-ing bird.

If that mocking bird won't sing,
Mama's going to buy you a diamond ring.

If that diamond ring turns brass,
Mama's going to buy you a looking glass.

If that looking glass gets broke,
Mama's going to buy you a billy goat.

If that billy goat won't pull,
Mama's going to buy you a cart and bull.

If that cart and bull turn over,
Mama's going to buy you a dog named Rover.

If that dog named Rover won't bark,
Mama's going to buy you a horse and cart.

If that horse and cart fall down,
You'll still be the sweetest baby in town.